National Income and Related Statistics for Selected Years, 1929-1993

*Billions of Dollars
**GNP data are presented for years prior of 1959

	1929	1933	1939	1941	1945	1950	1951	1952	1953	1954
**Basic National Income Accounts ** **										
Personal Consumption Expenditures*	77.3	45.8	67.0	80.8	119.6	192.1	208.1	219.1	232.6	239.8
Gross Private Domestic Investment*	16.7	1.6	9.5	18.3	11.3	55.1	60.5	53.5	54.9	54.1
Government Purchases*	8.9	8.3	13.6	25.0	83.0	38.8	60.4	75.8	82.8	76.0
Net Exports*	1.1	0.4	1.2	1.5	-0.5	2.2	4.5	3.2	1.3	2.6
SUM TO: Gross Domestic Product***	103.9	56.0	91.3	125.5	213.4	288.3	333.4	351.6	371.6	372.5
MINUS: Depreciation Allowance*	9.9	7.6	9.0	10.3	12.4	23.6	27.2	29.2	30.9	32.5
EQUALS: Net Domestic Product	94.0	48.4	82.3	115.2	201.0	264.7	306.2	322.4	340.7	340.0
MINUS: Indirect Business Taxes*	9.3	9.0	11.1	12.5	18.4	24.6	28.9	30.9	34.1	33.7
EQUALS: National Income	84.7	39.4	71.2	102.7	182.6	240.1	277.3	291.5	306.6	306.3
MINUS: Social Security Contributions	0.3	0.3	2.2	2.8	6.3	7.4	8.8	9.3	9.6	10.6
MINUS: Corporate Income Taxes*	1.4	0.5	1.4	7.6	10.7	17.9	22.6	19.4	20.3	17.6
MINUS: Undistributed Corp. Profits*	2.4	-4.1	0.3	2.3	4.4	8.2	8.8	9.6	8.6	9.8
PLUS: Transfer Payments*	3.7	3.7	4.8	4.1	9.8	21.8	19.4	20.5	22.4	24.8
EQUALS: Personal Income	84.3	46.4	72.1	94.1	171.0	228.4	256.5	273.7	290.5	293.1
MINUS: Personal Taxes*	2.6	1.4	2.4	3.3	20.8	20.6	28.9	34.0	35.5	32.5
EQUALS: Disposable Income	81.7	45.0	69.7	90.8	150.2	207.8	227.6	239.7	255.0	260.6
REAL GDP (in $1987 Billions)	709.6	498.5	716.6	909.4	1354.8	1203.7	1328.2	1328.2	1435.3	1416.2
Real Per Capita Disposable Income ($1982)	$3,923	$2,771	$3,834	$4,686	$5,991	$5,653	$5,651	$5,742	$5,964	$5,941
Annual Percent Change in Per Capita DI	0.0	-2.1	7.9	7.7	0.2	6.8	0.0	1.6	3.9	-0.4
Money and the Price Level										
Consumer Price Index (1982-4=100)	17.1	12.9	13.9	14.7	17.8	24.1	26.0	26.5	26.7	26.9
Percentage Inflation Rate	0.0	-5.1	-1.4	5.0	2.3	1.3	7.9	1.9	0.8	0.7
Supply of Money, M1*	26.3	19.2	33.3	45.0	98.7	115.6	122.2	126.8	128.2	131.6
Population / Labor Force										
Population (Millions)	121.8	125.6	130.8	133.4	139.9	152.3	154.9	157.6	160.2	163.0
Civilian Labor Force (Millions)	49.2	51.6	55.2	55.9	53.8	62.2	62.0	62.1	63.0	63.6
Unemployment (Millions)	1.6	12.8	9.5	5.6	1.0	3.3	2.1	1.9	1.8	3.5
Percent Unemployment / Total Labor	3.2	24.9	17.2	9.9	1.9	5.3	3.3	3.0	2.9	5.5
International Trade										
Exports*	7.1	2.4	4.6	6.1	7.4	14.5	19.8	19.2	18.1	18.8
Imports*	5.9	2.1	3.4	4.7	7.9	12.3	15.3	16.0	16.8	16.3
The Federal Budget										
Federal Government Receipts*	3.9	2.0	6.3	8.7	45.2	39.4	51.6	66.2	69.6	69.7
Federal Outlays*	3.1	4.6	9.1	13.7	92.7	42.6	45.5	67.7	76.1	70.9
Federal Surplus (+) or Deficit (-)*	0.7	-2.6	-2.8	-4.9	-47.6	-3.1	6.1	-1.5	-6.5	-1.2

Economics

Sixth Edition

Ralph T. Byrns

University of Colorado, Boulder

Gerald W. Stone

Metropolitan State College of Denver

HarperCollinsCollegePublishers

Acquisitions Editor: Bruce Kaplan
Developmental Editor: Mimi Melek
Project Coordination and Text Design: Innodata Corporation
Cover Designer: Sheila Stoneham
Cover Illustration: Steve Karchin
Art Studio: ElectraGraphics, Inc.
Manufacturing Manager: Willie Lane
Printer and Binder: R.R. Donnelley & Sons Company
Cover Printer: The Lehigh Press, Inc.

Economics, Sixth Edition

Library of Congress Cataloging-in-Publication Data

Byrns, Ralph T.
    Economics/Ralph T. Byrns, Gerald W. Stone, Jr.
6th ed.
        p.   cm.
    Includes index.
    ISBN 0-673-99316-7. (student edition)
    ISBN 0-673-99869-X (instructor's edition).
    1. Economics.   I. Stone, Gerald W.   II. Title.
HB171.5.B99   1995
330—dc20   94-48159
                                                                 CIP

95   96   97   98   9   8   7   6   5   4   3   2   1

Brief Contents

The following is a cross-reference to the chapters in *Economics* (hard-cover edition) and *Macroeconomics* and *Microeconomics* (the two paper-back editions).

		Chapter Number	
	Economics	*Macro-economics*	*Micro-economics*
Part 1 **Cornerstones of Economics**			
Economics: The Study of Scarcity and Choice	1	1	1
Scarcity in a World in Transition	2	2	2
Demand and Supply	3	3	3
Markets and Equilibrium	4	4	4
Part 2 **The Macroeconomic Environment**			
Foundations of Macroeconomics	5	5	
Employment and Unemployment	6	6	
Inflation	7	7	
Measuring Economic Performance and Growth	8	8	
Part 3 **Foundations of Macroeconomic Theory**			
Classical Macroeconomics and Keynesian Aggregate Expenditures	9	9	
Macroeconomic Equilibrium	10	10	
Fiscal Policy	11	11	
Part 4 **The Financial System**			
Money and Banking	12	12	
Central Banking: The Federal Reserve System	13	13	
Monetary Theory and Policy	14	14	
Budget Deficits and Public Debt	15	15	
Part 5 **Challenges to Macroeconomic Policymaking**			
Microfoundations of Macroeconomic Policy	16	16	
Active vs. Passive Policymaking	17	17	
Limitations of Stabilization Policy	18	18	
Economic Growth and Development	19	19	

		Chapter Number		
		Economics	*Macro-economics*	*Micro-economics*
Part 6	**Core Concepts in Microeconomics**			
	Elasticity	20		5
	Consumer Choice	21		6
	Theory of the Firm	22		7
	Production and Costs	23		8
Part 7	**Product Markets**			
	The Competitive Ideal	24		9
	Monopoly	25		10
	Imperfect Competition and Strategic Behavior	26		11
	Antitrust and Regulation	27		12
Part 8	**Resource Markets**			
	Competitive Labor Markets	28		13
	Imperfect Competition in Labor Markets	29		14
	Rent, Interest, Profits, and Capitalization	30		15
	Income Distribution and Poverty	31		16
Part 9	**Modern Microeconomic Issues**			
	Market Failure and Public Finance	32		17
	Public Choice	33		18
	Environmental Economics	34		19
	The Economics of Health Care	35		20
Part 10	**The International Economy**			
	International Trade	36	20	
	International Finance	37	21	21

Detailed Contents

To the Instructor   xxix
To the Student   xxxiv
Acknowledgments   xxxvii

Economics

Part 1   Cornerstones of Economics   3

Chapter 1   Economics: The Study of Scarcity and Choice   4

Scarcity   5

Production and Resources   6   Unlimited Human
Wants   8   Some Basic Choices   10   Opportunity
Costs   11   Monetary (Absolute) Prices   12
Economic Efficiency   14

Economic Analysis   16

Common Sense and Theory   16   Positive vs. Normative
Economics   18   Macroeconomics and
Microeconomics   19

*Chapter Review: Key Points   21

*Questions for Thought and Discussion   22

Optional Material: Graphical Techniques in Economics   23

Graphical Analysis   23

Cartesian Coordinates   23   Descriptive Graphs   24
Analytical Graphs   24   The Misuse of Graphs   28
Applications   29

Focus 1   Is Self-Interest Immoral or Unavoidable?   9

Focus 2   Is Life Priceless?   13

Chapter 2   Scarcity in a World in Transition   32

Circular Flows of Income   32

Households   33   Firms   33   Government   34

Specialization and Trade   35

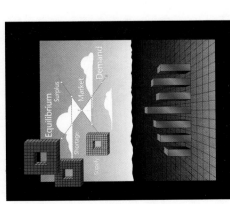

*Chapter Review: Key Points and Questions for Thought and Discussion appear
in every chapter.

v

Division of Labor 35   Comparative Advantage 35

Production Possibilities 37

Production Possibilities Frontiers 37   Diminishing
Returns 39

Economic Growth 41

Technological Advances 41   Expanding the Resource
Base 43   Growth and International Trade 46

Allocative Mechanisms 47

The Market System 47   Brute Force 47
Queuing 47   Random Selection 48   Other
Tradition 48   Government 48

Economic Systems in Transition 50

Foundations of Capitalism 50   Central Planning in a
Command Economy 52   Economic Systems as Information
Processors 53   Are Economic Systems Converging? 53

Focus 1   Is the United States at a Comparative
           Disadvantage? 38

Focus 2   Innovation, Entrepreneurship, and Economic
           Growth 42

Chapter 3   Demand and Supply 58

Thinking at the Margin 58

Demand 59

The Law of Demand 60   The All-Else-Being-Equal
(*Ceteris Paribus*) Assumption 60   Individuals' Demand
Curves 61   Market Demand Curves 63   Other
Influences on Demand 65   Changes in Demand 67
Changes in Quantity Demanded vs. Changes in Demand 68

Supply 69

The Law of Supply 70   Other Influences on
Supply 71   Changes in Supply 72   Changes in
Quantity Supplied vs. Changes in Supply 75

Market Equilibrium 75

Supplies and Demands Are Independent 78

Focus 1   Substitution and the Uses of Water as Its Price
           Changes 61

Biography   Alfred Marshall: Tools That Simplify Analysis 62

Focus 2   Expectations and Opportunity Costs 74

Chapter 4 Markets and Equilibrium 81

The Search for Equilibrium 81

Changes in Supply 82   Changes in Demand 83
Shifts in Supply and Demand 84

Transaction Costs 87

Intermediaries 87

Markets and Public Policy 89

Price Controls 89   Minimum Wages and
Unemployment 92   The War on Drugs 94

The Market in Operation 95

What? 95   How? 96   For Whom? 96

Government in a Market Economy 96

Providing a Stable Legal Environment 98   Promoting
Competition 98   Providing for Public Wants 98
Income Redistribution 99   Stabilizing Income, Prices,
and Employment 100

The Scope of Government 100

Biography Adam Smith: Father of Economics 83

Macroeconomics

Part 2   The Macroeconomic Environment   105

Chapter 5   Foundations of Macroeconomics   106

Business Cycles 107

Turning Points in Business Cycles 108   Social Aspects
of the Business Cycle 108

Business Cycle Theories 109

External Shock Theories 109   Population Dynamics
Theories 109   Marxian Capitalistic Crises 110
Long Waves and Innovations 111   Psychological
Theories 112   Classical Macroeconomic
Theory 113   Keynesian Theory 113

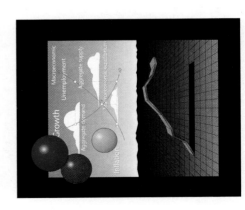

Aggregate Demand and Aggregate Supply   114

Aggregate Demand Curves   114

Shifts of Aggregate Demand Curves   115

Consumer Spending (C)   115   Investment (I)   117
Government (G)   118   The Foreign Sector (X − M)   118

Aggregate Supply   119

Slope of the Aggregate Supply Curve   119   Shifts in
Aggregate Supply   121

Macroeconomic Equilibrium   124

The American Business Cycle   125

The Prosperous 1920s   125   The Great Depression of
the 1930s   126   War and Its Aftermath in the
1940s   128   The Sluggish 1950s   128   The
Booming 1960s   128   Stagflation in the 1970s   128
The Erratic 1980s   128   Muddling Through in the
1990s   130

**Biography   Joseph A. Schumpeter: "Creative Destruction" and
Growth   112**

Chapter 6   Employment and
Unemployment   133

Labor Markets in the Twenty-First Century   133

Changes in the Supply of Labor   134   Changes in the
Demand for Labor   135

The Concept of Unemployment   137

Voluntary vs. Involuntary Unemployment   139   Sticky
Wages   140

Measuring Unemployment   141

Limitations of Unemployment Statistics   142

Sources of Unemployment   142

Frictional Unemployment   142   Seasonal
Unemployment   144   Structural Unemployment   144
Cyclical Unemployment   144   Induced
Unemployment   145   Accounting for Joblessness   146

The Duration of Unemployment   146

Costs of Unemployment   148

Losses of Aggregate Income   148   Social Costs of
Unemployment   148

Benefits from Unemployment **149**

Allocative Benefits 149   Disciplinary Benefits 150

Focus 1   How Can You Compete in a Global Economy? **138**

Focus 2   Part-Time Unemployment? **143**

Focus 3   Overqualified for the Job? **148**

Chapter 7   Inflation   153

The Concept of Inflation   **154**

Price Index Numbers   **154**

Measuring Consumer Prices (CPI) 154   How the CPI Is
Used 155   Problems with the CPI 157   Other
Price Indices 158

The History of U.S. Inflation   **159**

Types of Inflation   **160**

Creeping or Galloping Inflation vs. Hyperinflation 160
Anticipated vs. Unexpected Inflation 161   Demand-
Side Inflation 161   Supply-Side Inflation 162
Mixed Theories of Inflation 163

Inflation's Costs and Benefits   **164**

Real-Income Costs of Inflation 164   Social Costs of
Inflation 166   Benefits of Inflation 167   The
Discomfort Index 167

Focus 1   Is the CPI Biased as a Payment Escalator?   **157**

**Focus 2   Economies in Transition: Inflation and
Structural Change** 162

Chapter 8   Measuring Economic
Performance and
Growth   170

Gross Domestic Product (GDP)   **170**

GDP as an Economic Indicator 171   GDP and
Economic Well-Being 171

Measuring GDP   **172**

The Expenditure Approach 173   The Income
Approach 175

Reconciling GDP and NI   **177**

The Value-Added Technique 177

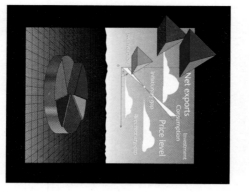

Part 3   Foundations of Macroeconomic Theory

191

Chapter 9   Classical Macroeconomics and Keynesian Aggregate Expenditures

192

Aggregate Expenditures   211

Biography   John Maynard Keynes: Father of Modern Macroeconomics   197

Chapter 10   Macroeconomic Equilibrium   215

Aggregate Expenditures and Equilibrium   215

National Output   216   Aggregate Expenditures   216   Keynesian Equilibrium   216   Price vs. Quantity Adjustments   218

A Keynesian Saving = Investment Equilibrium   218

Planned Saving and Investment   219   Balancing Planned and Actual Saving and Investment   220

The Multiplier Effect   220

The Great Depression: The Multiplier in Action   222   The Paradox of Thrift   224   The Investment Accelerator   226

Equilibrium Below Potential GDP   226

Potential GDP   226   The GDP Gap   227   The Recessionary Gap   227   The Inflationary Gap   228

Aggregate Demand and Aggregate Expenditures   228

Price Levels and Aggregate Expenditures   229   Shifts in Aggregate Demand Curves   229   Aggregate Demand and GDP Gaps   230

Optional Material: Graphical Techniques in Economics   234

Focus 1   Does Saving Stimulate Growth or Drag It Down?   225

Chapter 11   Fiscal Policy   235

Fiscal Policy: The Demand Side   236

Discretionary Spending and Equilibrium   236   Taxes and Equilibrium   237

Automatic Stabilizers   241

Automatic Tax Adjustments   241   Automatic Changes in Government Outlays   242

Cyclical vs. Structural Deficits   243

Classical Economics and Fiscal Policy   245

Does Taxation Have a National Limit?   245   Tax Revenue and Progressive Marginal Tax Rates   247   Government Purchases and Transfers: New Classical View   247

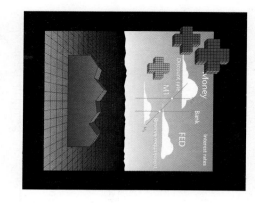

Federal Reserve Bank Districts   282   Organization of
the Fed   283

Tools of the Fed   283

Reserve Requirements   283   Open-Market Operations
(OMO)   285   Discounting Operations   287   The Fed's Secondary Tools   288   Which Tools Are
Used?   289

Financial Institutions in Transition   290

The Fed's Independence Under Attack   293

Proposals to Reform the Fed   293

**Focus 1   The Go-Around: An Expansionary Open-Market
Operation   287**

Focus 2   The Collapse of Savings and Loans   292

Focus 3   Stop-and-Go Fed Policies   294

Chapter 14   Monetary Theory and
Policy   297

The Demand for Money   297

Transactions Demands   298   Precautionary
Demands   299   Asset Demands   299   The Costs
of Holding Money   301

Classical Monetary Theory   302

The Equation of Exchange   303   The Crude Quantity
Theory of Money   303   The Classical View of
Investment   306   Classical Monetary
Transmission   306

Keynesian Monetary Theory   308

The Asset Demand for Money   308   The Keynesian
View of Investment   310   Keynesian Monetary
Transmission   311   Keynesian Analysis of Depressions
and Inflations   311

Monetarism   313

The Demand for Money Revisited   313   Determinants
of the Demand for Money   313   The Stability of the
Demand for Money   315   The Monetarist Monetary
Transmission Mechanism   315

Summary: Classical, Keynesian, and Monetarist Theories   316

Monetary Policy vs. Fiscal Policy   317

Relative Effectiveness Arguments   317   Rules vs.
Discretionary Policies   319   The Culpability of the
Fed   321   The Failure of Discretionary Fine-
Tuning   321

New Classical Economics and New Keynesian Economics   323

Focus 1   **Velocity on the International Scene   305**

Biography   **Milton Friedman: The Rebirth of
Monetarism   314**

Chapter 15   Budget Deficits and
Public Debt   326

Recent Growth of Deficits and Debt   327

Private vs. Public Finance   328

Private Budget Constraints   328   Local Government
Budget Constraints   328   The Federal Budget
Constraint   329

Functional Finance vs. Balanced Budgets   331

Balancing Budgets Annually   331   Budget Balancing
Over Business Cycles   331   Functional Finance   331

Crowding Out   333

Government's Costs When Resources Are Idle   333
Government's Costs During Full Employment   335

Federal Deficits and Foreign Trade   336

Trade Deficits   337

The Public Debt   337

External vs. Internal Debt   338   Interest on Public
Debt   339   Burdens on Future Generations   341
Must the National Debt Be Repaid?   341   Some Benefits
of Public Debt   342   Remeasuring Public Debt and
Budget Deficits   342   International Comparisons of
Debt   344

The Ability to Control Government Spending   345

Focus 1   **Ricardian Equivalence and Inflationary Finance   332**

Focus 2   **Will Social Security Absorb Our National Debt?   343**

Part 5   Challenges to Macroeconomic Policymaking   353

Chapter 16   Microfoundations of Macroeconomic Policy   354

The Aggregate Demand Curve   354
Slope of the Aggregate Demand Curve   354   Shifts in Aggregate Demand   357

The Aggregate Supply Curve   357
National Output and the Work Force   357   Shifts in Aggregate Supply   360

Unemployment   363
Labor Contracts   363   Efficiency Wages   364
Dual Labor Markets   365

Shocks to Aggregate Demand and Aggregate Supply   366
Demand-Side Inflation   366   Supply-Side Inflation   368   The U.S. Economic Record   371

Focus 1   Macroeconomics and Presidential Elections   370

Chapter 17   Active vs. Passive Policymaking   379

Trade-Offs Between Unemployment and Inflation   379
Shifts in Aggregate Demand: A Stable Trade-Off?   381
Supply Shocks and Unstable Phillips Curves   382

Keynesian Phillips Curves   383
The Keynesian Structuralist Approach   383   Structural Shocks and Wage-Price Stickiness   384   A Keynesian Theory of Stagflation   385

The New Classical Natural Rate Theory   387
The Natural Rate of Unemployment   388   Wage Adjustments to Inflation   388   The Long-Run Phillips Curve   389

The Natural Rate of Interest   391

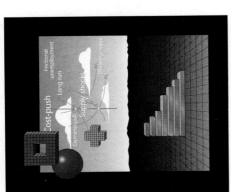

The Natural Real Rate of Interest Hypothesis 391
Keynes and Fisher Effects 392

New Classical Macroeconomics 392

Competitive Markets 396

Efficient Markets 396   Rational Expectations 396
Real Business Cycles 400

Biography **Irving Fisher: The Birth of Modern Monetary
Theory** 395

Focus 1 **Rational Expectations and Hyperinflation** 399

Chapter 18   Limitations of Stabilization Policy   404

Lags, Doses, and Stabilization 406

Recognition Lags 406   Administrative Lags 406
Impact Lags 406   Destabilizing Effects of Policy
Lags 407   Overdosing or Undermedicating a Sick
Economy 409

Insulation Against Monetary Policymaking 410

Political Dimensions of Macro Policy 412

Political Business Cycles 412   Has Keynesian Theory
Induced Government Growth? 415

Are Recessions Engineered to Decompress Inflation? 416

Recessions to Discipline Labor 416   Policymakers'
Abhorrence of Recessions 417

Incomes Policies to Combat Inflation 417

Evaluation of Incomes Policies 418

A Brief Evaluation of Policy Rules vs. Discretion 419

Biography **Ludwig von Mises and Friedrich A. Hayek: Austrian
Economics** 405

Focus 1 **Internationalization and Macroeconomic
Policy** 413

Chapter 19   Economic Growth and Development   423

Economic Growth 423

How Are Economic Growth and Development Related? 424
Aggregate Demand, Aggregate Supply, and Economic
Growth 424

Sources of Economic Growth   **425**

Land and Natural Resources   425   Population and
Labor Force Changes   426

Saving, Investment, and Capital Formation   428

Voluntary Saving   429   Involuntary Saving   431
Capital Widening and Deepening   432   Technological
Advances   433   Social Foundations: The Infrastructure   435

Development and the Unfolding of History   436

Economic Development According to Marx   436
Stages of Economic Growth   438

Problems of Developing Nations   440

The Trap of Underdevelopment   440
Breaking the Bonds of Underdevelopment   440
Is There Really a Trap of Underdevelopment?   441
How Developed Countries Can Aid Less Developed
Nations   442   The Role of International Credit   443

Focus 1   Growth and the Rule of 72   425

Focus 2   Can Government Stimulate Technology?   434

Biography   Karl Marx: Revolutionary Socialism   437

Focus 3   Economic Development and Political Freedom   439

Microeconomics

**Part 6   Core Concepts in
Microeconomics   447**

Chapter 20   Elasticity   448

Elasticity and Responsiveness   448

The Price Elasticity of Demand   449

The Problem of Bases and Percentages   449
Ranges of Elasticity   450   Elasticity and Total
Revenue   451   Elasticity Along a Demand Curve   454
Determinants of Elasticity of Demand   454
Other Elasticities of Demand   456

The Price Elasticity of Supply   458

Supply Elasticities and Time   459

Elasticity and Tax Burdens   459

Tax Incidence   459   Summary: Taxes and
                            Elasticity   463

Chapter 21   Consumer Choice   466

Commodities and Services   466

Utility   467

Total and Marginal Utility   467   The Law of
Diminishing Marginal Utility   470

Consumer Equilibrium and Demand   470

Maximizing Utility   471   Balancing Marginal
Utilities   471   Price Adjustments and Marginal
Utility   472   Effects of Price Changes   473
Consumer Surplus   474   The Paradox of Value   475

Information and Rational Choice   477

Goods as Bundles of Attributes   477   Uncertainty and
Imperfect Information   477   The Bewildering Maze of
Choices   478   Quality and Prices   479

Asymmetric Information   480

Moral Hazard   480   Adverse Selection   481
The Market for Lemons   481   Consumer Policy   482

Optional Material: Graphical Techniques in Economics   484

Budget Lines   484   Indifference Curves   485
Consumer Equilibrium   486   Deriving Individual
Demand Curves   487   Income and Substitution
Effects   487

Biography   Jeremy Bentham: The Birth of
            Utilitarianism   468

Focus 1   Rational Ignorance and Artificial Intelligence   472

Biography   Thorstein B. Veblen: Status and the Leisure
            Class   478

Chapter 22   Theory of the Firm   490

Modern Business   490

Production   492   The Short Run and the Long
Run   492   Plants, Firms, and Industries   492

Why Do Firms Exist? 493

Reducing Transaction Costs 493   Economies of Scale and Scope 494

Legal Forms of Business 495

Sole Proprietorships 496   Partnerships 496
Corporations 496   Other Forms of Enterprise 497

Financing Business Operations 498

Financial Intermediation 498   Self-Financing and
Retained Earnings 498   Common Stock 499
Corporate Bonds 499   Loans from Financial
Intermediaries 500

Business Goals 500

Profit Maximization 500   Normal Profits as Production
Costs 501   Other Business Goals 502

Problems Facing Business Organizations 502

Separation of Ownership and Control 502   Market Pressures
The Principal–Agent Problem 502   503
and Evolution 503

Focus 1   So You Want to Be an Entrepreneur? 494

Focus 2   Reengineering: Take a Clean Sheet of Paper 505

Chapter 23   Production and Costs   509

Production Functions 509

Production in the Short Run 510

Marginal and Average Physical Products of Labor 510
The Short-Run Law of Diminishing Marginal
Returns 512

Short-Run Production Costs 513

Fixed Costs 513   Variable Costs 514   Average
Costs 515   Marginal Costs 517   Relating Costs
to Production 518

Costs in the Long Run 521

Least Cost Production 521   Long-Run Average
Costs 522   Economies and Diseconomies of
Scale 523   Economies of Scope 523
Measuring Long-Run Average Costs 523

Technological Change 525

Part 7 Product Markets 533

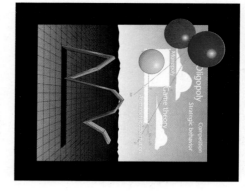

Chapter 24 The Competitive Ideal 534

Market Structures 534
The World of Pure Competition 535
　Competition vs. Rivalry 536
Short-Run Competitive Pricing and Output 537
　Total Revenue – Total Cost Approach 537
　Marginal Revenue = Marginal Cost Approach 538
　Short-Run Supply 545
Long-Run Adjustments in Purely Competitive Industries 548
　Economic Profits as Market Signals 548　　The Process of
　Competition 549　　Long-Run Equilibrium in a Purely
　Competitive Industry 550　　Long-Run Industry Supply
　Curves 552
Evaluating Competitive Markets 554
　Economic Efficiency 555　　Social Welfare 555
　Decentralized Decisions and Freedom 556
　Some Shortcomings of Market Economies 556
**Focus 1 Dynamic Entrepreneurs vs. Competition: The Austrian
　School** 557
**Biography Leon Walras and Vilfredo Pareto: General
　Equilibrium and Welfare Analysis** 558

Chapter 25 Monopoly 561

Monopoly Markets 561
　Market Power 563
Monopoly Pricing and Output 564
　Barriers to Entry 570
Price Discrimination 573
　Requirements for Price Discrimination 573
　Profits from Price Discrimination 574
Competitive vs. Monopolized Markets 575
　Differences in Prices and Outputs 576
　The Inefficiency of Monopoly 577
　Price Discrimination and Efficiency 578
　Monopoly and Inequity 578

Biography   Antoine Augustin Cournot: Foundations of Modern Game Theory   562

Focus 1   Patents, Trademarks, Copyrights, and Piracy   571
Focus 2   Arbitrage and Price Discrimination   574

Chapter 26   Imperfect Competition and Strategic Behavior   581

Product Differentiation   582
Monopolistic Competition   584
   Short-Run Pricing and Output   585   Long-Run Adjustments   585   Resource Allocation and Efficiency   586
Oligopoly   587
   Mutual Interdependence   587   The Origins of Oligopoly   587   Oligopolistic Decision-Making   588   Evaluating Oligopoly   592
Game Theory   593
   Strategy in Game Theory   594   Prisoners' Dilemma   594   Cooperation in Game Theory   595   Moving First   596   Dynamic Games   596   Asymmetric Payoffs   597
Strategic Behavior in Business   598
   Contestable Markets   598   Predatory Behavior   599   Limit Pricing   601   Sunk Costs as Entry Barriers   601   Accommodation   603

Biography   Joan Robinson and E.H. Chamberlin: Bringing Realism to Theories of Market Structure   583

Chapter 27   Antitrust and Regulation   606

The Structure-Conduct-Peformance Paradigm   606
Measuring Market Power   607
   The Lerner Index of Monopoly Power   607   Market Concentration Ratios   608   The Herfindahl-Hirschman Index   608   Difficulties in Categorizing Industries   610
Mergers and Market Power   610
   Major Merger Movements   610   Is Concentration Increasing?   611   Is Big Bad?   612   Public Policies Toward Business   613

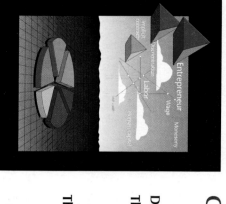

Part 8   Resource Markets   635

Antitrust Policy   614
The Antitrust Laws   615   Exemptions from Antitrust
Laws   616

Antitrust in Practice   617
Monopolization and Market Power   617
Merger Policy   618   Trends in Antitrust   618

Regulation   620
The Growth of Government Regulation   620

Theories of Regulation   621
The Public Interest Theory of Business Regulation   623
Industry Interest Theory of Regulation   626
Public Choice Theory of Regulation   628

Perspectives on Regulation   628
Direct Costs of Regulation   628   Indirect Costs of
Regulation   628   Deregulation and Reregulation   629

**Biography   George Stigler: The Changing View of
Regulation   619**

Chapter 28   Competitive Labor Markets   636

Derived Demands for Resources   636

The Demand for Labor   637
Marginal Revenue Product   637   Value of the Marginal
Product   637   Shifts in Demands for
Labor   638   Elasticity of Demand for Labor   640

The Supply of Labor   640
Population and Labor Force Participation   641   Labor
vs. Leisure Choices   641   Wage Structures and
Rates   643   Human Capital   643   Wage
Structures and Labor Supplies   647

Labor Market Equilibrium   648
Marginal Factor Cost   648   Profit Maximization and
Employment   648   Wages and
Employment   649   Labor Market Efficiency   650

Strategic Behavior in Labor Markets   650
Implicit Labor Contracts   651   Screening and
Signaling   653   Efficiency Wages   653

Wage Differentials   655
Wage Differentials and Discrimination   655